Butterflies Move Freely
Exploring Immigration in the USA & beyond

Elias Benjelloun
Published by Butterflies Move Freely
Las Vegas, NV
Phone: (702) 551-4965
Email: info@butterfliesmovefreely.com
www.butterfliesmovefreely.com

ISBN 9798333982872

Printed in the United States of America
First Printing 2024
First Edition 2024

10 9 8 7 6 5 4 3 2 1

DEDICATION

IN TRIBUTE TO OUR PARENTS, WHO BROUGHT US TO THIS LAND OF OPPORTUNITY WITH SACRIFICE,

IN RECOGNITION OF THE LEADERS WHO CAME BEFORE US, WITH VISION AND COURAGE,

DEDICATED TO THE KIDS, WHO WILL INHERIT AND INSPIRE THE WORLD AFTER US,

AND FOR ALL THE BUTTERFLIES IN THE WORLD, STRIVING TO FIND A PLACE TO CALL HOME AND BUILD.

TOGETHER, LET US CHART A COURSE FOR UNITY, PROSPERITY, AND FREEDOM.

BUTTERFLIES MOVE FREELY

ELIAS BENJELLOUN

Meet A Butterfly, Elias Benjelloun

Elias Benjelloun is a passionate advocate for immigrant rights, a tech entrepreneur committed to social impact and community development.

Born to immigrant parents, his journey began when his family sought refuge in the United States, shaping his commitment to social justice.

Graduating high school at 14 as the "Vegas Whiz Kid," Elias studied Biology at UNLV, where he became the youngest Student Body President and initiated various scholarship, academic, and advocacy programs for students.

Elias founded Tech Start, empowering people with technology—from kids learning new skills to young adults building careers, and small businesses, nonprofits, and government agencies implementing cutting-edge tech.

His personal experiences, particularly during the Trump administration's immigration policies, have strengthened his resolve to fight for immigration reform and human rights. Through his book, Butterflies Move Freely, Elias champions a united and inclusive society.

Having grown up in Las Vegas, Elias continues to lead his entrepreneurial ventures and advocate for social justice, aiming to make a lasting impact on the world for future generations.

Join The Movement

www.ButterfliesMoveFreely.com

PREFACE

Why am I writing this?

My ultimate goal is to instill a renewed sense of unity and interconnectedness among us all.

I hope we exchange empathy and compassion.
I hope we transcend past tribalism.
I hope we embrace our shared humanity.

I believe that once you've finished reading this, you will feel a deeper sense of understanding and be uniquely compelled to take action.

What does immigration mean to you?
Mark this book up and express what you feel...

____

____

____

____

____

____

Table of Contents

A History of Shattered Bonds 01

Dreams of a United Humanity 10

Comic: Accepting Xander 23

A Historic Snapshot of US Immigration Policies 37

UNITED 53

Comic: Catching Yara 61

Yeehaw to FML: Growing Up Unsure in America 67

So What Now? 77

Charting Paths Forward with LOVE 83

Comic: Becoming Zophia 89

True Immigrant Values 95

Thank You 99

Collection of Quotes 101

Summer 2017

I got a phone call and I felt my world and all my dreams shatter in an instant.

Join The Movement

www.ButterfliesMoveFreely.com

A History of Shattered Bonds

A History of Shattered Bonds

A mother with her children, their fingers intertwined, sob in uncontrollable agony.

They reach out for each other, their faces etched with helplessness of heartache and a despair too profound to be described by mere words.

They lose their tightest grip, are ripped apart and put in separate lines, destined to individual futures alone.

Not too far away in another line, their father watches on... if he's lucky.

They are defeated in this bitter reality.

A family shattered.

This heartrending spectacle is not a standalone event but a recurring theme in history where powerful empires tear apart families under the guise of nationalism.

No matter which country or era, these government-forced separations predominantly target marginalized communities, evoking haunting echoes of the past.

Elias Benjelloun

When we concede and reduce to our greatest fears as human beings, unrelenting trauma & death follows.

The story of Jewish migration to Europe is a tale as old as time (70 CE).

Since the Roman Empire and throughout European history Jews have immigrated for a variety of reasons, including religious persecution, economic opportunities, and political upheaval.

Let us remind ourselves that one of humanity's darkest moments festered from fear, racism, and persecution.

When the Nazis came to power in 1933, they implemented a series of discriminatory laws and policies targeting Jews.

These included the Nuremberg Laws, which stripped Jews of their citizenship and introduced segregation and persecution.

Over time, the persecution escalated, leading to the implementation of the "Final Solution," the systematic extermination of six million Jews during the Holocaust.

Millions of families were shattered.

The trauma experienced by these individuals and communities still reverberates through generations.

Similar echoes can be heard along concentration camps around the world.

In the Southern border of the United States families are separated every day for the sake of immigration control.

However, these are not the only instances.

George Santayana

Those who cannot remember the past are condemned to repeat it.

These are not the only instances...

United Kingdom | 2018 - Present
The United Kingdom implemented a policy known as the "Windrush Scandal" in recent years. It affected individuals who arrived in the UK from Commonwealth countries before 1973.

Due to changes in immigration laws, many individuals were wrongfully detained, denied legal rights, and faced deportation. As a result, families were separated, with some members being forcibly removed from the country.

Australia | 1990s - Present
Australia has had a controversial policy of mandatory immigration detention for asylum seekers arriving by boat.

Under this policy, individuals, including families, are detained in offshore processing centers while their refugee claims are assessed. This has resulted in the separation of families, with adults and children being held in separate detention facilities.

These are not the only instances...

Israel | 1950s - Present
In the context of the Israeli-Palestinian conflict, Israel has implemented policies that have led to the separation of Palestinian families. This includes the construction of a separation barrier/wall, restrictions on movement and residency, and the revocation of residency rights for certain individuals. These policies have resulted in families being divided, separated and most recently at its worst, genocidal.

Africa | 1990s - Present
Certain regions in Africa, particularly war-torn areas like Uganda, have suffered greatly under ruthless warlords and armed groups. The Lord's Resistance Army (LRA), led by Joseph Kony, stands as a chilling example. Operating through extensive child abduction campaigns, the LRA conducted nighttime raids, killing parents and leaving children exposed to abduction. Thousands of children, some as young as six, were forcibly taken and subjected to unimaginable horrors as child soldiers, porters, and even sex slaves.

Similar instances of child abduction and recruitment have been seen in conflict-ridden regions worldwide, such as Sierra Leone, the Democratic Republic of Congo, Sudan and South Sudan, the Central African Republic, and Myanmar, where children have been forcefully taken, coerced, or recruited into armed forces, enduring unimaginable suffering and a loss of their childhood innocence.

These are not the only instances...

Chile | 1970s
In the 1970s, under the brutal dictatorship of Augusto Pinochet, many Chilean families were torn apart.

Children were often taken from their parents, who were deemed enemies of the state, and relocated to politically sympathetic families.

Australia | 1910 - 1970s
Australia's Stolen Generations, which occurred between 1910 and the 1970s, saw Aboriginal and Torres Strait Islander children forcibly removed from their families by Australian Federal and State government agencies and church missions.

This misguided policy, aimed at assimilating these children into the dominant Western culture, tore apart communities and disrupted generational bonds.

United States (Japanese Internment) | 1940s
During World War II, the United States implemented policies that resulted in the forced internment of Japanese-Americans.

Following the attack on Pearl Harbor, Japanese-Americans, including many U.S. citizens, were relocated to internment camps. This policy led to the separation of families and the infringement of their civil liberties.

These are not the only instances...

South Africa (Apartheid) | 1900s
During the era of apartheid in South Africa, the government implemented strict racial segregation policies that forcibly separated families.

Non-white South Africans were subjected to the Group Areas Act, which designated specific areas for different racial groups. Families were forcibly removed from their homes and relocated to racially segregated areas, resulting in family separations.

Canada | 1800s - 1900s
In Canada, the late 19th and 20th century witnessed the forced assimilation of indigenous children through the residential school system.

This practice aimed at eradicating indigenous cultures and identities resulted in thousands of children being forcibly separated from their families.

Spain | 1492
Similarly, during the Reconquista in Spain, which culminated in 1492, Jews and Muslims were expelled from the Iberian Peninsula if they did not convert to Christianity.

Families were often separated in the ensuing chaos, with many children left behind or lost during the difficult journeys to safer lands.

These are not the only instances...

Mongol Empire | 1200s
One such example can be found in the expansion of the Mongol Empire in the 13th century. As the Mongols conquered various regions, they often forcibly relocated large numbers of people, including skilled artisans and craftsmen, to other parts of their empire.

These forced migrations would have inevitably led to family separations, as those deemed valuable were moved, leaving others behind.

These examples highlight a grim side of our collective history. It is a tale of the forceful imposition of power, the dominance of one group over another, and a stark reminder of the lasting psychological trauma inflicted upon the vulnerable.

This haunting testament to the enduring pain caused by government-forced separations spans different eras and regions.

These stories reveal a recurring pattern of fear, prejudice, and systemic injustice.

As you continue to read this book, I hope you will look past fear and hate-driven narratives and commit to a love-based approach.

See immigrants for who they truly are: fellow humans striving for a brighter future for their families.

Let us learn from the past and strive for a more compassionate and just world.

Dreams of a United Humanity with Individual Liberty for All

Dreams of a United Humanity with Individual Liberty for All

I dream of a united humanity, where every person is cherished, and individual liberty is upheld.

I envision a world where love and unity are the pillars that uphold us.

Let's kindle empathy within ourselves and accept each other with open hearts. In a world often divided by differences, our ability to embrace and understand one another becomes our strength, never a weakness.

Let's nurture this profound interconnectedness that binds us. We are stewards of this fragile planet, in a delicate dance with existence.

Empowered by individual liberty, our actions and choices affect not only ourselves but also the broader human family and the environment we all share, for generations to come. We are interconnected, and together, we are stronger.

Together, we can strike a balance where personal freedom and social responsibility coexist harmoniously.

This dream embraces equity and empowerment for all. Let's take action by providing resources and support to unlock the limitless potential within each individual.

By ensuring everyone has access to opportunities and the means to succeed, we create a more just and prosperous world for all.

Diversity adorns this dream of mine.

It's our unique differences that bring us together.

The varied cultures, beliefs, and perspectives enrich our collective life experience and foster innovation and growth that lead to even greater prosperity for all.

I declare my unwavering commitment to realizing this Dream of a United Humanity with Individual Liberty for All.

Let's celebrate this richness, recognizing that our strength lies in our unity amid diversity.

Let's challenge our biases and stereotypes, overcome our fears, and pave the way for a future grounded in unity and mutual respect.

In this united world, every voice is heard, every individual is valued, and every dream is possible.

Let us work together to turn this vision into reality, one step at a time, for the betterment of all humanity.

I declare my unwavering commitment to realizing this Dream of a United Humanity with Individual Liberty for All.

Join us on this passionate quest for love of all the good things... unity, interconnectedness, liberty, equity, empowerment, diversity, and inclusion.

Cultivating Love & Unity

In a world that often seems fractured and divided, cultivating love and unity is not just an aspiration but a fundamentally important mission.

Accepting one another and embracing unity are essential values that define our shared humanity. This is particularly important in the context of immigration, where individuals leave their homelands in search of new opportunities, safety, and refuge.

Immigration reminds us of the interconnectedness of our global community, as people from diverse backgrounds come together seeking a better life and contributing to the cultural and economic fabric of their adopted homes.

When we open our hearts to understanding and accepting immigrants, we tap into the power of empathy and compassion. We recognize that their journeys are often filled with hardships, sacrifices, and the pursuit of dreams.

By embracing immigrants with love and unity, we extend a welcoming hand, providing a supportive environment that acknowledges their inherent worth and the contributions they bring to our societies.

In the face of divisive rhetoric and prejudices surrounding immigration, our commitment to unity becomes even more vital.

Cultivating Love & Unity

We reject the notion of "us versus them" and instead celebrate the richness and diversity of us all. We recognize that our destinies are intertwined, and the success of one is intertwined with the success of all.

By cultivating love and unity, we foster an environment where immigrants are not just tolerated but embraced and valued.

We challenge misconceptions and create inclusive spaces where their unique experiences, talents, and perspectives are recognized and celebrated.

We advocate for policies that promote fair and compassionate immigration systems, ensuring that individuals are treated with dignity and respect throughout their journeys.

In this united front, we create a society that thrives on the strength of our diversity, where the contributions of immigrants are celebrated as a source of enrichment.

Together, we build bridges across cultures and transcend boundaries, uniting in our shared humanity. By cultivating love and unity, we create a world where immigration is not a source of division but a testament to our collective progress and humanity.

Let us commit to this mission, starting with our own actions and attitudes. Together, we can make a difference, one act of love and unity at a time.

Nurturing Interconnectedness and Liberty

In our quest for a more unified world, we must nurture interconnectedness and uphold the principles of liberty, for they are the twin pillars that shape our collective destiny.

We recognize that individual liberty is not a privilege reserved solely for citizens, but a fundamental right inherent to all humans.

It is a flame that must be protected and kindled within every heart, allowing individuals to express themselves freely, pursue their passions, and contribute to the greater tapestry of humanity.

Individual liberty is the fundamental right of each person to live freely, making choices without undue government oppression.

This principle is at the heart of democratic societies, emphasizing personal freedom, autonomy, and the pursuit of happiness. Our interconnectedness highlights how our lives and freedoms are linked with those of others.

By understanding and valuing individual liberty, we can better appreciate the need to recognize these unalienable rights for everyone, including immigrants. These rights are inherent from birth and should not be denied based on nationality or immigration status.

By nurturing interconnectedness and liberty, we create a world where every individual is recognized, respected, and valued.

Nurturing Interconnectedness and Liberty

However, immigrants often face severe challenges that undermine their liberties. Many lack legal due process, facing expedited deportations and having limited or no path to residency or citizenship.

Additionally, immigrants are more likely to be exploited for labor, working under harsh conditions and low wages, often out of fear of deportation.

By recognizing their individual liberty and our interconnectedness, we can build a better society.

This recognition enriches our communities, bringing diverse cultural, social, and economic benefits that enhance our society.

By embracing the liberty and human rights of immigrants, we uphold our values of freedom and equality.

Individual liberty and interconnectedness strengthens our community and fosters a more inclusive and vibrant environment for all.

Establishing Equity and Empowerment

In our unwavering pursuit of a more just and inclusive world, we must prioritize equity and empowerment as fundamental principles.

By building a society grounded in equity, we strive to dismantle barriers and create a fair playing field where opportunities to build and contribute to our society are accessible to all, regardless of immigration status.

Establishing equity for immigrants is exemplified when we advocate for fair policies that ensure every individual, regardless of their background, has an equal chance to succeed.

This includes providing access to quality education and in-state tuition for undocumented students, eradicating a huge barrier that has hindered so many students from progress.

Equity is realized when immigrants have the ability to obtain work permits, can compete for scholarships, and even access safe and affordable housing.

This allows Butterflies to contribute to the economy, support their families and help create safer communities.

The journey toward a united humanity begins with equity, but it also compels us to empower each other.

Empowerment is about fostering the inherent potential within every individual and cultivating an environment where their talents can flourish.

Establishing Equity and Empowerment

Empowerment is the process of enabling individuals to realize their full potential by providing the tools, opportunities, and support needed to thrive.

It involves fostering an environment where every person can develop their talents and contribute meaningfully to society.

Imagine how much safer, organized, and successful the process becomes for all stakeholders when empowerment takes center stage?

Mentorship becomes a powerful tool, guiding and supporting immigrants as they navigate their personal and professional journeys.

We all know that mentors can offer valuable insights, help build networks, and provide the encouragement needed to overcome challenges.

Scholarships open doors to education, enabling immigrants to unlock their potential and pursue their dreams. Access to higher education and vocational training equips immigrants with the skills necessary to thrive in the job market.

Business and work opportunities, including the ability to secure work permits, provide avenues for growth and self-sufficiency.

Empowering immigrants with the right to work legally helps them contribute to the economy and support their families, fostering financial independence and stability.

Establishing Equity and Empowerment

Guidance and support systems are instrumental in fostering empowerment, ensuring that no one is left behind. Yet, this is often an after-thought to existing policies.

Providing resources such as language classes, job placement services, and legal assistance helps immigrants integrate and succeed.

When Butterflies succeed, the entire ecosystem thrives, benefiting communities and economies alike.

> **Imagine how much more successful the process becomes when empowerment takes center stage?**

It's commonly misunderstood that immigrants are unlawfully bypassing immigration rules.

However, the reality is that for most undocumented Butterflies, there are no available and feasible legal routes or immigration laws that facilitate their path to residence and citizenship due to a complicated and restrictive system.

Pathways to residency and citizenship are crucial for this vision of Butterflies Move Freely.

Establishing clear, fair, and accessible routes to legal status allows immigrants to fully participate in society and contribute to its development.

These pathways create a more equitable and empowering society.

Celebrating Diversity and Inclusion

Our vision celebrates diversity that enriches our humanity, recognizing that, deep within us, we are all immigrants.

From the earliest days of human history to the present, migration has been a core part of the human journey, binding us together through shared experiences of seeking new beginnings.

Each wave of migration has shaped our societies, contributing to the growth, innovation, and cultural richness we enjoy today.

By honoring the contributions of Butterflies, we celebrate their resilience, unique perspectives, and the immeasurable value they bring to our communities.

We must move beyond the divisive notion of "us versus them" and embrace the reality that our destinies are interconnected. Fear and tribalism have long been obstacles to unity, fostering division and misunderstanding.

To overcome these barriers, we must work together to dismantle stereotypes and biases, replacing them with a culture that honors and embraces the diversity of cultures that form our collective humanity.

The stories of Butterflies are so diverse. Lets give a platform to these voices, sharing their stories, aspirations, and dreams.

Celebrating Diversity and Inclusion

Inclusivity means creating an environment where every individual feels valued, respected, and has equal access to opportunities and resources.

It is about acknowledging and celebrating our differences while fostering a sense of belonging for everyone. We are all part of the equation of inclusivity the moment we were born.

In our journey toward a more united and inclusive world, let us embrace diversity and inclusion as guiding principles.

Let us celebrate the colors, cultures, and contributions that Butterflies bring to society.

As we build a more inclusive society, we recognize our responsibility extends beyond our borders. We advocate for just and compassionate immigration policies, acknowledging the shared responsibility to protect the rights and dignity of all individuals, regardless of their country of origin.

Through community engagement initiatives, such as cultural festivals and educational workshops, we foster mutual respect and understanding, breaking down the walls of fear and prejudice.

By working together, we eliminate fear and tribalism, creating a world where the inherent worth and contributions of immigrants are recognized and celebrated. Let us celebrate the colors, cultures, and contributions that Butterflies bring to society.

Celebrating Diversity and Inclusion

By acknowledging our shared humanity, we cultivate love and unity, establish equity and empowerment, nurture interconnectedness and liberty, and celebrate diversity and inclusion.

In unity, we find our strength; in equity, our fairness; in interconnectedness, our common ground; and in diversity, our true richness.

Let us create a future that honors these ideals, ensuring that the spirit of Butterflies thrives in a world of compassion, opportunity, and boundless potential for all.

JOIN US | Dreams of a United Humanity with Individual Liberty for All

Through this manifesto, we declare our unwavering commitment to realizing our dreams of a united humanity with individual liberty for all.

We march forward, brought here by our varied heritage, fueled by the values of love, unity, interconnectedness, liberty, equity, empowerment, diversity, inclusion, and acceptance.

Each action we take, no matter how small, brings us closer to transforming our dream into reality.

Together, we shall create a world where every person, whether an immigrant or native-born, is valued, liberated, and cherished.

It is in this world that the bonds of our united humanity grow stronger, where our collective journey is enriched by the diverse contributions of immigrants from all corners of the globe.

Accepting Xander

Accepting Xander

Xander had always felt out of place on his home planet. As a member of the Nulian race, he possessed telekinetic abilities that set him apart from most of his peers. When he heard about Earth's United Federation of Planets, he saw an opportunity to start anew.

When he arrived on Earth, Xander found it difficult to adjust to the different customs and cultures of his new home.

He struggled to communicate with the humans, who did not possess telepathic abilities like some Nulians. Despite the challenges, Xander was determined to make a new life for himself.

He found a job at a local cafe and began to explore the city on his days off. Slowly but surely, he started to make friends with the humans he met. He discovered a love for Earth music and even joined a band.

However, Xander's biggest challenge came when he met Jennifer. She was a human woman who he had grown to care for deeply.

But when he revealed his story as a Nulian, Jennifer struggled to accept him. She had grown up with preconceptions about aliens, and Xander's telekinetic abilities made her uncomfortable.

Xander was heartbroken. He had hoped that Earth would be a place of acceptance and inclusion, but he had been met with fear and suspicion. He didn't know how to convince Jennifer that he was just like her in so many ways.

Accepting Xander

Meanwhile, tensions were rising in the city due to a spate of terrorist attacks. A group of extremist humans had been targeting and attacking aliens, believing that they were a threat to humanity. Xander's Nulian community was feeling increasingly threatened, and many were considering leaving Earth altogether.

Xander knew that something had to be done. He reached out to his human friends and together they organized a peace rally to show support for the intergalactic community.

Jennifer, despite her initial hesitations, joined Xander on stage and delivered a moving speech about the need for unity and understanding.

At the rally, Xander also spoke about his own experiences as an alien living on Earth. He talked about the challenges he had faced and how he had found acceptance among his friends and colleagues.

He urged the humans to see past their fears and embrace the diversity of the intergalactic community.

As the rally progressed, a group of extremist humans arrived, shouting insults and threats at the aliens and the humans who supported them. Xander was alarmed, but he didn't want to resort to violence.

Instead, he reached out to the attackers telepathically, trying to understand their anger and frustration.

Accepting Xander

Through deep interpersonal dialogue, Xander was able to see the attackers' fears and concerns.

They felt threatened by the presence of aliens on Earth, and they believed that the intergalactic community posed a danger to human society.

Xander listened to their concerns and tried to reassure them that they had nothing to fear.

He then walked up to the attackers, speaking openly and calmly. He acknowledged their concerns and explained that the intergalactic community was not a threat.

He urged them to see the similarities between humans and aliens and to embrace diversity and inclusion.

Slowly but surely, the attackers' anger began to dissipate. They saw Xander as a fellow human, despite his telekinetic abilities, and they were willing to listen to his words.

Xander's peaceful demeanor and empathetic approach had a profound effect on the attackers, and they eventually agreed to leave the rally peacefully.

The incident was a turning point for the city. Many of the humans who had previously harbored fears and prejudices began to see the aliens as fellow inhabitants of the planet.

Xander had played a pivotal role in promoting peace and unity

A Historic Snapshot of US Immigration Policies

A Historic Snapshot of US Immigration Policies

"The bosom of America is open to receive not only the opulent and respectable stranger, but the oppressed and persecuted of all nations and religions, whom we shall welcome to a participation of all our rights and privileges."
- President George Washington, 1783

In American history, the evolution of immigration policy stands as a testament to our nation's struggle toward a more inclusive and just society.

Over the years, pivotal legislation has shaped the lives of millions, reflecting the ebb and flow of our collective values and aspirations.

This chapter delves into several key transformative moments in US immigration policy, highlighting milestones that have significantly influenced the lives of countless individuals.

President
George Washington

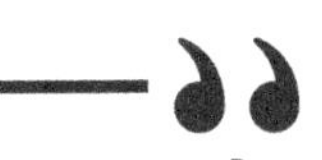

America is open to receive... the oppressed and persecuted of all nations and religions...

By examining these policies and their impacts, we hope to foster a better understanding of the complex history and attitudes around immigration.

A Historic Snapshot of US Immigration Policies

"As a nation, we began by declaring that 'all men are created equal.' We now practically read it 'all men are created equal, except Negroes.' When the Know-Nothings get control, it will read 'all men are created equal, except Negroes, and foreigners, and Catholics.'"
- President Abraham Lincoln, 1855

1965 | Immigration and Naturalization Act

The Immigration and Naturalization Act of 1965, also known as the Hart-Celler Act, marked a profound turning point in US immigration policy.

This landmark legislation abolished the earlier quota system that had limited immigration based on national origin and introduced a new framework centered on reuniting immigrant families and attracting skilled labor to our shores.

Its profound impact was felt across the nation as immigrants from Asia, Africa, and Latin America began to form an integral part of American society, growing our economy and enriching our culture.

President
Abraham Lincoln

As a nation, we began by declaring that 'all men are created equal.'

A Historic Snapshot of US Immigration Policies

"I believe in the idea of amnesty for those who have put down roots and who have lived here, even though sometime back they may have entered illegally." - President Reagan, 1984

1986 | Immigration Reform and Control Act (IRCA)

Under President Ronald Reagan, immigration policy experienced notable developments that left a lasting impact on the nation. In 1986, he signed the Immigration Reform and Control Act (IRCA) into law. This comprehensive legislation aimed to address the challenges posed by unauthorized immigration while simultaneously providing a pathway to legal status for certain undocumented immigrants.

The IRCA introduced employer sanctions, making it unlawful for employers to hire unauthorized workers knowingly. It also established a one-time amnesty program, enabling eligible undocumented immigrants who had been continuously present since 1982 to apply for legal status.

President
Rondald Reagan

I believe in the idea of amnesty for those who have put down roots and who have lived here...

The amnesty programs collectively granted amnesty to over 3 million individuals who had previously lived in the shadows.

A Historic Snapshot of US Immigration Policies

The 1990s was a pivotal decade for U.S. immigration policy. Several significant legislative efforts help shaped the nation's approach to immigration.

These acts built upon the foundations laid by earlier laws, reflecting a growing recognition of the value of diversity and the need for comprehensive reform.

1990s | A Decade of Immigration Acts

The 1990 Immigration Act further built upon the foundations laid by the Hart-Celler Act of 1965.

This legislation modified and expanded the earlier framework, increasing the overall level of immigration to 700,000 individuals annually. Its provisions also sought to increase the diversity of the immigrant flow by prioritizing the admission of individuals from underrepresented countries.

This emphasis on diversity reflected our growing recognition of the value and strength derived from embracing Butterflies from all walks of life.

"We should be increasing the number of legal immigrants, so that we can continue to build our economy and strengthen our families and communities." - President Clinton, 1995

During President Bill Clinton's tenure, immigration policy continued to evolve. In 1996, he signed the Illegal Immigration Reform and Immigrant Responsibility Act (IIRIRA) into law. This aimed to strengthen border security, streamline deportation processes, and address concerns related to welfare and public benefits for immigrants.

A Historic Snapshot of US Immigration Policies

The IIRIRA also introduced more stringent grounds for deportation and limited access to certain federal benefits for non-citizens.

It was aimed at restricting the liberties of Butterflies due to the fearful attitude surrounding immigration.

It established provisions that barred individuals who had accumulated certain periods of unlawful presence in the United States from re-entering the country for a specified period of time.

However, President Clinton also played a pivotal role in the passage of the Nicaraguan Adjustment and Central American Relief Act (NACARA) in 1997.

NACARA provided relief to certain individuals from Nicaragua, Cuba, El Salvador, and Guatemala who had faced various immigration challenges.

It granted them the opportunity to seek legal status and provided a pathway to permanent residency for those who met specific criteria.

These laws aimed to strike a balance between ensuring the integrity of our immigration system and upholding the principles of fairness and justice.

President
Bill Clinton

We should be increasing the number of legal immigrants, so that we can continue to build...

A Historic Snapshot of US Immigration Policies

The 2000s saw unprecedented challenges that underscored the need for comprehensive reform and a deepening divide that resulted in a seemingly never-ending deadlock.

2000s | A Decade of Turmoil

In the aftermath of the devastating events of September 11, 2001, our nation stepped into a time marked by increased scrutiny, discrimination, and profiling.

Folks from Muslim-majority countries found themselves under a magnifying glass, their lives altered by policies such as the National Security Entry-Exit Registration System, or NSEERS.

This created widespread fear and disrupted the lives of many individuals and families, raising major concerns and slippery slopes surrounding individual liberties and its balance with privacy and security.

President
George W. Bush

We're a nation of laws.. We're also a nation of immigrants... These are not contradictory goals.

America's southern border has been a hotspot of challenges. This isn't a simple issue. It's about more than just keeping our borders secure; it's also about the rights and lives of real people seeking refuge.

But in 2005, the country's attitude towards immigration took a further right turn.

A Historic Snapshot of US Immigration Policies

In 2005, the stage was set for Operation Streamline, a policy cloaked in the guise of criminal prosecution.

Its aim: to bring individuals caught crossing the border without proper documentation to face the full weight of the law. The goal was to deter illegal immigration by prosecuting individuals caught crossing the border without proper documentation.

This policy led to mass prosecutions and a substantial increase in detention rates, overwhelming the judicial system and highlighting its limited capacity to handle such cases efficiently.

The consequences of Operation Streamline were far-reaching. Families were often separated as individuals faced criminal charges and detention, causing emotional and financial strain on those affected.

"We're a nation of laws, and we must enforce our laws. We're also a nation of immigrants, and we must uphold that tradition, which has strengthened our country in so many ways. These are not contradictory goals. America can be a lawful society and a welcoming society at the same time."
President George W. Bush, 2006

A Historic Snapshot of US Immigration Policies

Although the DREAM Act was first introduced in 2001 by Senators Dick Durbin and Orrin Hatch, it did not gain significant momentum until the early 2010s.

2010s | Hope for Dreamers

Under President Obama's leadership, with support from Senator Harry Reid, the conversation around the DREAM Act intensified.

This legislative measure aimed to provide a pathway to conditional residency and, upon fulfilling additional requirements, permanent residency for qualifying undocumented minors.

"Are we a nation that accepts the cruelty of ripping children from their parents arms? Or are we a nation that values families? And works together to keep them together." - President Obama, 2014

The debate around the DREAM Act continued throughout the 2010s but the seemingly never-ending deadlock did not break.

Congress did not act and the immigration system continued to turmoil. The immigration system continued to struggle under the weight of outdated policies and increasing demands for reform.

Notably, President Obama took action via executive order with the introduction of DACA (Deferred Action for Childhood Arrivals) in 2012.

This policy represented a significant milestone in acknowledging the plight of individuals brought to the United States as children.

A Historic Snapshot of US Immigration Policies

DACA granted a renewable two-year period of deferred action from deportation and provided eligibility for work permits.

This program created a path for young individuals to pursue their dreams while contributing to society. Dreamers are able to work and pursue higher education, but still lack viable paths to permanent residency or citizenship.

President
Barack Obama

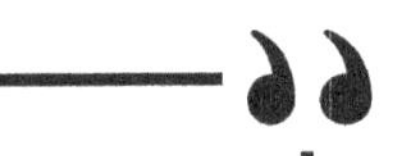

“Are we a nation that accepts the cruelty of ripping children from their parents arms? Or are we a nation that values families? And works together to keep them together.”

Reflect on your own legal status:

- If you're an immigrant, how would your life change with the rights of citizenship?
- If you're a citizen, how might your life change if you were an undocumented immigrant?

____

____

____

____

____

____

A Historic Snapshot of US Immigration Policies

The Trump administration ushered in a series of stringent anti-immigrant policies that profoundly impacted the lives of millions.

These policies, driven by a far-right agenda, emphasized national security while flagrantly disregarding the humanitarian and ethical implications.

Some of the key policies include Travel Ban, Family Separation Policy, ending DACA, Public Charge Rule, asylum restrictions, TPS revocations, ICE raids and constructing the border.

A Far Right Era of Anti-Immigrant Oppression

In the era of President Trump, we witnessed a series of executive actions that came to be known as the Trump Travel Ban.

This policy, which began with the executive order titled "Protecting the Nation from Foreign Terrorist Entry into the United States" in January 2017, marked a stark departure from our nation's long-standing tradition of welcoming those seeking refuge and a better life.

Labeled as the "Muslim ban" due to its disproportionate impact on majority-Muslim countries, the ban targeted several countries, including Iran, Libya, Somalia, Syria, and Yemen, among others.

It sparked a fierce debate about our nation's values, the balance between national security and human rights, and the very definition of who we are as humanity.

A Historic Snapshot of US Immigration Policies

My fellow Butterflies, we must remember that our strength lies in our diversity, in our shared commitment to the ideals of liberty, justice, and the pursuit of happiness.

Policies like the travel ban, which close our doors to the world, do not make us safer or stronger. Instead, they undermine our standing in the world and betray the core values that we, as a nation, hold dear.

We must strive for policies that uphold our values, embrace our diversity, and affirm our global leadership.

It's important to remember that the strength of our nation lies not in the fear of those who are different from us, but in our ability to embrace diversity and uphold the values that define us.

When we talk about keeping 'bad people' out of our country, we must be careful not to paint with a broad brush.

The vast majority of those seeking to come to our shores are not 'bad people' with 'bad intentions.' They are mothers and fathers, sons and daughters, seeking the same things we all want - safety, opportunity, and a better future for their families.

Yet, President Trump targeted these families directly.

In 2018, we found ourselves in the harsh glare of a heartbreaking reality, a humanitarian crisis unfolding right here on American soil.

A Historic Snapshot of US Immigration Policies

The Family Separation Policy, a measure intended to curb unauthorized immigration, left deep, lasting scars on the most vulnerable among us - our children seeking refuge.

It tore apart families, causing immeasurable pain and suffering.

However, this crisis has not ended and n 2023, we were confronted with a chilling revelation - our federal authorities had reportedly lost track of 85,000 migrant children!

This shocking news underscores the overwhelming issues facing the system and the pressing need for comprehensive immigration reform.

And we must also not lose sight of the many efforts led by the United States Immigration and Customs Enforcement, known as ICE, throughout the 2000s and beyond.

Large-scale deportations have cast a long shadow over our communities, impacting millions of undocumented immigrants and causing significant disruption.

Families are torn apart, communities are left trying to rebuild, and the effects ripple out far beyond our own borders and era.

If we fail to solve these ongoing growing challenges, then the consequences will be grave. The safety and well-being of children and communities are at risk.

We must do better, for the sake of our shared values and for the future of our humanity.

A Historic Snapshot of US Immigration Policies

"Immigration is essential to who we are as a nation, our core values, and our aspirations for our future."
- President Joe Biden, 2020

Defining History Today

As we reflect on the evolution of US immigration policies, we stand at a pivotal moment where we can define our future with compassion and forward-thinking reforms.

Our history has shown that inclusive and humane immigration policies lead to a more diverse, vibrant, and prosperous society. We must learn from these lessons and build on them to create a system that reflects our highest ideals.

Now is the time to address the reality of the 10 million undocumented immigrants living in the United States.

Providing amnesty and a clear, achievable path to citizenship for these Butterflies is not only a moral imperative but also a pragmatic solution that acknowledges their contributions and integrates them fully into our society.

By granting us a fair legal status, we can foster stronger communities, boost our economy, and uphold the values of justice and equality that are the bedrock of our nation.

Together, we can define our legacy as a nation that welcomes, empowers, and uplifts all who seek a better life within our borders.

A Historic Snapshot of US Immigration Policies

We must develop better systems to manage the influx of migrants seeking refuge and opportunity in the United States.

This includes creating humane asylum procedures, improving border management, and expanding legal immigration avenues. By doing so, we ensure a fair and orderly immigration system that benefits both migrants and our society.

Our nation's history shows the strength that comes from embracing immigrants. Let us commit to inclusive, just policies that reflect our core values.

Together, we can define our legacy as a nation that welcomes, empowers, and uplifts all who seek a better life.

President
Joe Biden

> **Immigration is essential to who we are as a nation, our core values, and our aspirations for our future.**

UNITED:
Uplifting Nations, Immigrant Talents Elevate Development

UNITED

UNITED stands for “Uplifting Nations,, Immigrant Talents Elevate Development.” This section highlights a handful of immensely positive contributions immigrants made to society.

When we are UNITED, we are wealthier, safer, and happier as a society.

The contributions of American immigrants span from the arts to the sciences, from business to public service, and have played an instrumental role in shaping the America we love today.

This is a tribute to the remarkable individuals and their indelible impact on our society.

Celebrating Immigrant Contributions:

- Alexander Hamilton, a founding father of the United States, was an immigrant born in Nevis. Yet, he served an extraordinary role in establishing our nation's financial system.
- Albert Einstein, a German immigrant, revolutionized our understanding of the universe with his theory of relativity.
- Elon Musk, hailing from South Africa, has pushed the boundaries of technology and space exploration with SpaceX and Tesla.
- Madeleine Albright, born in Czechoslovakia, shattered glass ceilings as the first woman to serve as U.S. Secretary of State.
- Sergey Brin, an immigrant from Russia, co-founded Google, transforming the way we access information.
- Andrew Carnegie, a Scottish immigrant, led the expansion of the American steel industry.

Celebrating Immigrant Contributions:

- Joseph Pulitzer, a Hungarian immigrant, made a lasting impact on journalism and literature.
- Leoh Ming Pei, a Chinese immigrant, designed iconic structures like the Louvre Pyramid, significantly impacting global architecture.
- Arianna Huffington, a Greek immigrant, co-founded The Huffington Post, transforming digital journalism and demonstrating the internet's power to engage citizens in democracy.
- Julissa Arce, an undocumented immigrant from Mexico, became a vice president at Goldman Sachs, exemplifying the resilience and contributions of immigrants.
- Dulce Matuz, an electrical engineer and immigrant rights advocate, was named one of Time's 100 most influential people in 2012. She co-founded the Arizona DREAM Act Coalition, showing immigrants' potential to lead and inspire change.
- Indra Nooyi, an immigrant from India, served as the CEO of PepsiCo, leaving a significant mark on the corporate world and highlighting immigrants' role in business innovation.

These individuals, and countless others, have brought their unique talents, perspectives, and resilience, enriching our society in immeasurable ways.

They remind us that America's strength lies in its diversity, in its ability to attract and nurture talent from around the world.

UNITED

The Role of Butteflies in America's Growth

As we navigate the complex and often contentious debate around immigration reform, let us remember these stories.

Every Butterfly, whether documented or undocumented, brings the potential to uplift our society, drive innovation, and contribute to our collective progress.

Across the nation and at scale, Butterflies contribute to America in many meaningful ways.

Butterflies, both documented and undocumented, are essential to our workforce, significantly contributing to both low-skilled and high-skilled occupations. They fuel industries like agriculture, construction, and hospitality while also advancing technology, science, and medicine.

Butterflies have an exceptional entrepreneurial spirit, leading over a quarter of all new businesses in the U.S. These ventures range from family businesses to groundbreaking tech startups, driving job creation and economic growth.

Their contributions are pivotal in innovation, accounting for over 75% of patents from the top 10 patent-producing universities.

Economically, Butterflies, including undocumented individuals, fulfill their tax obligations, contributing $11.74 billion annually to state and local economies.

UNITED

The Role of Butteflies in America's Growth

As consumers, Butterflies stimulate business activity and job creation through their demand for goods and services.

They fill labor gaps in critical sectors like agriculture, food service, and home health care, roles often unfilled by native-born Americans. Their contributions bolster Social Security and Medicare.

In 2014, immigrant households contributed $223.6 billion in federal taxes and $104.6 billion in state and local taxes, with first-generation immigrants adding $182.4 billion to Medicare and Social Security.

Our diversity is our strength. By embracing this diversity, we truly become UNITED.

Consider These Questions:

Were you aware of the extent of immigrant contributions before reading this? How does it affect your view on immigration policy?

____

____

____

____

____

____

Consider These Questions:

Can you trace the steps of your family's journey to where you are today?

Whether it was a generation ago or 20 generations ago, and regardless of whether your ancestors migrated from another region or have always lived in the same area, every family's history is a rich tapestry of experiences.

Share any stories or knowledge you have about your family's origins and movements.

____

____

____

____

____

____

____

____

____

____

____

____

____

____

Consider These Questions:

What cultural traditions and values might your family celebrate?

How have these traditions and values been preserved and passed down or started through generations in your family?

Consider These Questions

Catching Yara

Catching Yara

Yara was born and raised in Haiti. She had always dreamed of living in a place where she could have a better life, a place where she wouldn't have to worry about poverty, hunger, or violence.

When she heard about the opportunities in Venezuela, she decided to make the journey and start afresh.

Her parents had saved every penny they could to afford the journey for their daughter to escape to Venezuela, where they had heard there were better opportunities.

The day finally came when Yara was to leave. She bid farewell to her family and set off on the long and dangerous journey with a group of other Haitians seeking a better life.

They traveled on foot through treacherous terrain and dense forests. They were constantly on edge, wary of bandits, wild animals, and border guards.

Days blurred into weeks, the journey seemingly never-ending. They often went hungry and thirsty, with only small rations to sustain them.

At night, they cling to each other for warmth and safety in the dark of night, praying for safe passage into their newfound haven.

Finally, they reached the border of Venezuela.

But were met with corrupt border guards demanding bribes that they could not afford.

Catching Yara

They were turned away several times before finally finding a sympathetic guard who relented and let them cross.

Yara was relieved to be in Venezuela, but her troubles were not over yet.

She left everything behind and started anew in a strange land, full of unknown people and customs.

She had to learn a new language and adapt to a new culture. She remained resolute, poised to seize the opportunities awaiting her in this uncharted chapter of her life.

For a while, things were going well for Yara. She had found a job and was working hard to build a new life for herself.

She even applied to a small community college and was ecstatic when she was accepted. But then, things took a turn for the worse.

Yara was arrested at a college party and charged with drug trafficking, a crime she had not committed. The authorities didn't believe her protestations of innocence and sentenced her to 20 years in prison.

Yara had been arrested and charged with drug trafficking, a crime she had not committed. She was sitting alone in her cell, feeling hopeless and alone.

Suddenly, she heard a voice outside her cell. "Hey, you in there. What are you in for?"

Catching Yara

Yara looked up to see a woman standing outside her cell. She was a fellow inmate, and she looked friendly enough.

"I was framed," Yara replied, trying to keep her voice steady.

"Ah, I see," the woman said. "That's rough. What's your name?"

"I'm Yara," she replied.

"I'm Maria," the woman said, smiling. "Listen, Yara, you can't give up hope. You have to keep fighting, no matter how hopeless it seems. I've seen people get out of here before, people who were in worse situations than you. You just have to keep pushing and never give up."

Yara was touched by Maria's words. She had been feeling so alone and helpless, but Maria's words gave her a glimmer of hope.

"Thank you," Yara said, feeling a lump form in her throat.

"Don't mention it," Maria replied. "We've got to stick together in here."

Yara knew that Maria was right. She couldn't give up hope. She had to keep fighting, no matter how hard things got.

It wasn't until years later that Yara found out she had been framed by one of her classmates.

Catching Yara

The classmate, who was white, had smuggled drugs into the party and had purposely left them in Yara's possession. When the drugs were discovered, Yara was the only Black student in the room, and so she was blamed for the crime.

For the first few years, Yara struggled to adjust to life in prison. She was surrounded by dangerous criminals, and she feared for her safety. But gradually, she learned to navigate the prison culture and make friends with other inmates.

Over time, Yara became known for her kindness and her willingness to help others. She tutored other inmates who were struggling to learn to read and write, and she helped those who were sick or injured. Yara was determined to make the most of her time in prison and to use it to help others.

As the years went by, Yara began to lose hope. She knew that she had been wrongly convicted, but she couldn't see a way out. She missed her family and her homeland, and she longed to be free.

Finally, in 2022, after 20 long years, Yara was released from prison. She was overjoyed to be reunited with her family and to breathe the fresh air of freedom once again.

But she was also filled with a sense of sadness and loss. She had lost so much during her time in prison, and she knew that she could never get those years back.

Yara decided to use her experience to help others.

From Yeehaw to FML: Growing Up Unsure in America

From Yeehaw to FML: Growing Up Unsure in America

"Look Ma! Look what I got" a South Carolina boy called out surrounded by fellow young kids as he opened his birthday gifts.

This 5 year old kid with a Southern zeal and a darker than usual summer tan grew up where the sunrise inspired early outdoor fun, a day full of dedicated studies, and church on Sundays.

Oftentimes this kid and his family were welcomed to the front of the congregation to share testimonials, read and contribute to the conversation around faith and acceptance.

That same kid traded homework help for skateboard tricks in the neighborhood and when needed, bully prevention at school.

These are some of my earliest memories growing up in America. I never really thought of myself as anything other than an American.

However, it wasn't always sunshines growing up in America. Tornadoes were frequent enough—both the literal storms that swept through our neighborhoods and the unexpected struggles we faced as immigrants, which we will get to soon.

President
Barack Obama

Being an American is not a matter of blood or birth... It's a matter of faith... Anybody can help us write the next great chapter in our history

From Yeehaw to FML: Growing Up Unsure in America

"Being an American is not a matter of blood or birth. It's a matter of faith. It's a matter of fidelity to the shared values that we all hold so dear. That's what makes us unique. That's what makes us strong. Anybody can help us write the next great chapter in our history." - President Obama 2010

I pledged allegiance to the American flag just like every other student growing up here. My parents raised me with the core values of hard work, education, and contributing back to society. These values are shared among many Americans and immigrants alike.

As my parents moved our families to different states pursuing new work and business opportunities, we exemplified those core values: my parents worked hard, I studied hard, and in whatever small ways we would contribute to society. My parents' hard work paid off at times throughout their careers and they employed hundreds of Americans as a result, on top of providing for our family. I studied hard and fell in love with the pursuit of knowledge. It was that passion that fueled me, not the traditional school system itself. But because we traveled so much throughout my childhood I experienced a full spectrum of the American school system. I went to public schools, private schools, was homeschooled, and finished high school online.

Along the way and as a result of homeschool, I was mandated to take a state administered test to measure my grade level. To everyone's surprise at ~11 years old I was testing at a high school grade level.

This afforded me the opportunity to enroll in an online high school and start earning credits. I accelerated through the program and at 14 graduated high school earning the title by local news as the "Vegas Whiz Kid."

The following year in 2010, my pursuit of knowledge led me to the University of Nevada, Las Vegas (UNLV), where I studied Biology, inspired by a dream of serving others with medicine.

I gained early academic success one summer contributing to research projects that lead to publication. As a teenager I became a chapter author in a microbiology research textbook and contributor to various scientific projects. These early accomplishments filled me with excitement, solidifying my passion for learning and discovery.

Outside of the quiet labs where we explored biochemistry, microbiology, and neuroplasticity - I started to fall in love with student life. Student life led me to various roles on campus organizing with student groups focused on academic success, scientific research, community service, and civic engagement.

My various roles including President, Co-Founder, Secretary and really active member to several organizations led me to so many serendipitous opportunities. My favorite is the time I was invited to meet President Barack Obama when he visited our campus in 2012. Not too long after, I became the youngest Student Body President at UNLV and was able to help steward various programs.

My contributions include the funding of UNLV's first Undergraduate Research Center, hundreds of student scholarships, professional development programs, tons of events, and advocating for students on issues related to college affordability, campus safety, housing and more.

While juggling my own pursuit of knowledge, thru studies, research, and leadership - I constantly struggled to afford college tuition.

As an immigrant, I was mostly ineligible for scholarships at the time. Every semester was a juggle to pay tuition or face being dropped out of school. It was the support from my family and community combined with my own hard work that paid my way through college. While I had all of that support, paying tuition out of pocket was still a major challenge for me back then and there were many times I was about to get kicked out due to non-payment.

I was always a problem solver and that made me very entrepreneurial. Earlier on it was flipping video games and trading cards. Eventually I realized that I could monetize my digital technology skills and started earning opportunities to deliver websites and social media campaigns oftentimes for $1,000 per project.

It was these digital skills that really made the difference in earning my way through college and being hyper competitive for the work opportunities I was able to get. These skills uniquely positioned me to kickstart my career and contribute meaningfully to community projects.

From Yeehaw to FML: Growing Up Unsure in America

“If you don’t pay your past-due tuition by tomorrow at 5PM, you’ll be kicked out of classes and removed from your office as student body President,” the administrators told me. They were just doing their jobs and my mind was racing thousands of thoughts per second.

“Oh the embarrassment.. the failure... and in my last semester,” I thought to myself seeing my life go down another path completely. Thankfully, because of my hard work, support of my family, and the generosity of community leaders I was able to see college thru and be the first in my family to walk that graduation stage.

After college, I realized that my passions were rooted in entrepreneurship, technology, education, and community. I was able to join a community that combined all of these passions in Downtown Las Vegas at a magical place known as Llamapolis or commonly known as the Airstream Park.

This unique community was founded and owned by Tony Hsieh, the billionaire founder of Zappos and the Downtown project. Tony's innovative spirit and dedication to fostering connections left a lasting impact on everyone he met, including myself. His legacy continues to inspire us all.

I was surrounded by high-caliber entrepreneurs and in the midst of the downtown scenes. I got the startup bug here and got involved in many entrepreneurial projects, mainly focused around education and innovation. While most failed at that time, it was an adventure filled with learnings and opportunities.

From Yeehaw to FML: Growing Up Unsure in America

One opportunity led to joining the Uber team launching the Vegas market, the next opportunity led to joining a political agency as their Digital Director, with many side hustles and projects along the years.

Then in 2017, with all of the paid learning experiences I was ready to relaunch my startup and created "Tech Start for Kids." Through collaborations with public and private schools and UNLV we impacted the lives of over 300 students, unlocking these kids' potential through the power of education.

My work with Tech Start for Kids was going so well that my startup was scheduled to receive a $50K award from the National Science Foundation to discover best practices and deliver the model nationally.

But that opportunity never came to fruition...

One faithful day as I was starting my work at the office, I got a phone call and I felt my world and all my dreams shatter in an instant.

My Mom called me, her voice broken and scared: "Your sister was detained by ICE and we need you now!"

Then we learned that my family was being targeted for removal and we were next. The Trump Administration deemed hardworking, motivated and decent families like mine as criminals.

From Yeehaw to FML: Growing Up Unsure in America

Overwhelming feelings of shame, estrangement and loss took over me for the years to follow. "I thought I was American, how did this happen?"

My family's start in America is marked by pending asylum status that spanned nearly 20 years.

In June 1998, my parents embarked on a courageous journey, seeking a better future for their family in America as asylum refugees.

While the specifics of that pivotal moment escape my memory (I was 2 years old), the weight of their sacrifice and the dreams they nurtured have always been with me.

Mom

"Your sister was detained by ICE and we need you now!"

Life has a peculiar way of shaping us, taking us on unexpected journeys that can defy all logic and challenge our very sense of belonging.

In approximately 2010, my father, the owner of a popular on-strip hookah lounge reported a tip to the FBI.

After nearly 20 years of battling court cases, it seemed like a breakthrough when, seemingly overnight, they took over our immigration case with a promise of redemption.

But like many Arab immigrants in America, he bore the weight of exploitation by law enforcement: valued for his expert contributions but ultimately left abandoned when he was no longer deemed necessary.

The consequences were swift and devastating. With no active immigration case in the court system along with broken promises, our deportation order arrived swiftly after Trump's election, casting a dark cloud over our hopes and dreams that followed us to this day.

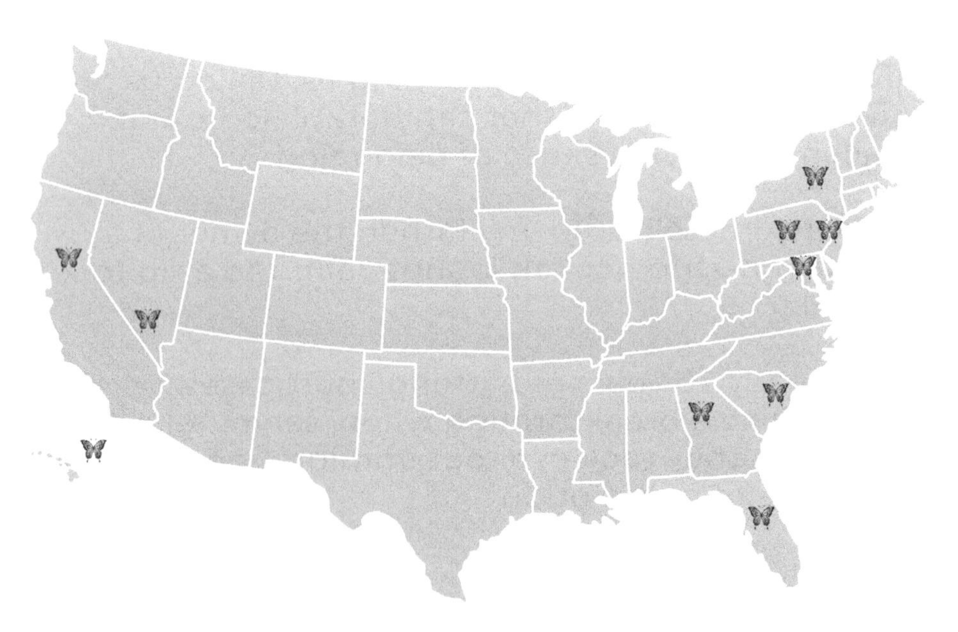

So What Now?

So What Now?

Ultimately, I just want to cross the border and hug my Mom. Ideally without triggering a permanent bar and abandoning the life I built here in the US.

The immigration system, as it stands, is built on exclusion rather than the inclusive values America was founded on.

It's time for comprehensive immigration reform rooted in love, not fear.

The current system's complexity and lack of accessible legal pathways have trapped many like me, creating barriers that are often insurmountable and marred by stripped liberties.

Growing up under pending status, I unknowingly accrued unlawful status when I turned 18. This was a technicality that we were never made aware of until it was far too late, and that has had profound implications for my legal standing.

When my family and I left the country on the advice of the FBI to avoid immediate deportation, we inadvertently triggered a 10-year bar, further complicating our situation.

These issues—accrued unlawful status at 18 and the 10-year bar triggered by leaving the country—made my sponsorship case impossible, resulting in its denial. Despite submitting all the necessary paperwork and following the proper procedures, these legal barriers rendered my case untenable.

So What Now?

Even though I grew up here, I lack any substantial paths to citizenship just like millions of other New Americans longing to be recognized at home.

In response to these challenges, I am committed to helping change the narrative, empower fellow community-loving immigrants and new Americans like myself to find a path to citizenship. This initiative is not just about fighting an exclusionary legal system; it's about ensuring that those who contribute positively to our communities can be accepted by the place they call home.

My goal is to provide the necessary resources and support to immigrants also trapped by an often unforgiving immigration process, ensuring they have the opportunity to stay, thrive in their communities and be returned their civil liberties.

This is about more than just my case—it's about advocating for a fairer, more compassionate approach to immigration and more broadly the world.

The funds raised by this book will help advocate for new solutions, help cover legal fees, provide expert counsel, and support Butterflies who have made positive contributions to society but are trapped by the current system's limitations.

So What Now?

We need an immigration system that reflects the realities faced by immigrants and embraces inclusivity. Simplifying the process to gain legal status and citizenship, expanding protections like DACA, and creating clear paths for those under Temporary Protected Status (TPS) or Deferred Enforced Departure (DED) are essential.

Our laws should recognize the vital contributions that immigrants make to our economy and culture, making it easier to obtain work permits, access higher education, and receive healthcare.

Addressing safety within the context of immigration policy is critical and by Integrating immigrants more effectively into our society enriches our communities and also enhances safety.

When immigrants are not forced into the shadows by harsh or confusing policies, they are more likely to cooperate with law enforcement and community leaders to help maintain public safety. This cooperation can be essential in identifying and addressing potential threats quickly, ensuring that those who pose real risks are dealt with appropriately.

It's important to recognize that the vast majority of immigrants care deeply about their communities.

We work hard, contribute to the local economy, and uphold values that support communal growth and safety. By reforming our immigration laws to focus on acceptance and integration, we not only uphold the values of justice and equity but also promote a safer society for everyone.

So What Now?

By comprehensively reforming the immigration system, we can create a path that truly matches the ethos of a nation built by immigrants.

These changes will make our system not just more logical and effective but also fairer and more humane, benefiting all of us who call this country home.

Join me in advocating for comprehensive immigration reform that reflects the true values of America.

Support the establishment of the legal aid fund to help immigrants navigate the complexities of the system and secure their place in the communities they call home.

Together, we can create a future built on unity, compassion, and shared prosperity.

Join The Movement

Butterflies Move Freely

Charting Paths Forward with LOVE:

Liberty, Opportunity & Value for Everyone

Charting Paths Forward with LOVE:
Liberty, Opportunity & Value for Everyone

In this vast and diverse country of the United States, the notion of America as a land of opportunity has always been a beacon of hope.

Yet, as our nation grapples with the complex issue of immigration, we must confront the fact that our current system falls short of upholding the principles that have made this country great.

Elias Benjelloun

It is time to chart a new path forward, one guided by the values of LOVE: Liberty, Opportunity, and Value for Everyone.

Love is not a passive emotion; it is an active force that propels us to understand and uplift one another. It is the driving force behind our pursuit of justice and equality. And when we extend that love to those who have migrated to our lands and shores, we create a society that is stronger, richer, and more compassionate.

Liberty is the cornerstone of our nation, and it demands that we protect the rights and freedoms of all individuals. Regardless of their origin or immigration status.

It means treating each person with dignity and respect, recognizing that their dreams and aspirations are as valid as our own.

**Charting Paths Forward with LOVE:
Liberty, Opportunity & Value for Everyone**

We must ensure that our immigration system reflects this commitment to liberty, providing a fair and just pathway for those seeking refuge, reunification with loved ones, or simply a chance to contribute to our society.

Opportunity is the lifeblood of America, the promise that with hard work and determination, anyone can achieve their full potential. We cannot turn our backs on the countless individuals who arrived with nothing but a pocketful of dreams.

By embracing comprehensive immigration reform, we unlock the untapped potential of millions, empowering them to contribute their skills, talents, and innovative spirit to our shared future.

Value for Everyone means recognizing that our collective success is intrinsically linked to the well-being of every individual. When we marginalize and exclude members of our society, we not only diminish their humanity but also stifle the vibrant tapestry of ideas and experiences that make us who we are.

By fostering a culture of inclusivity and belonging, we create a nation that thrives on diversity and understands that our strength lies in our unity.

We're Better Together.

Charting Paths Forward with LOVE:
Liberty, Opportunity & Value for Everyone

Achieving these ideals require us to come together as a nation and demand for comprehensive immigration reform. Don't shy away from the complexity of the issues or allow fear and prejudice to cloud our judgment.

Instead, let's approach this challenge with compassion, abundance, and a commitment to shared prosperity.

A Comprehensive Approach to Immigration Reform

We are at a critical juncture and it's critical to embrace comprehensive approaches to reform.

We can combine our capacity for compassion and abundance with a commitment to justice and create a system that can be an example for the world.

Our immigration system must reflect our values as well as the realities and needs of the modern world. This includes rethinking the current lottery and border migration systems to create a more inclusive and merit-based approach. It makes sense that the immigration system should consider a broader range of factors, such as intentions, willingness to work, education, skills, and family ties. This way we can create a fairer and more effective system that attracts individuals who can contribute to our economy and enrich our society.

There are over 11 million undocumented individuals living in the United States, most of whom, especially Dreamers, are contributing positively to their communities.

Charting Paths Forward with LOVE: Liberty, Opportunity & Value for Everyone

Creating a clear and accessible pathway to citizenship is not just a matter of restoring civil liberties but also an investment in our country's future. Implementing fair and reasonable processes that allow Butterflies to earn their citizenship through background checks, taxes, and positive contributions is a common sense approach to immigration policy. It will unlock many new skills, talents, and perspectives and usher in greater prosperity for all.

As a leader in the world, the United States has a responsibility to set a positive example for other nations navigating immigration policy. We can pioneer a path towards prosperity by balancing security concerns with humanitarian values. Let's encourage a global dialogue that respects the dignity and rights of all individuals.

Let us build a system that upholds the values of LOVE, ensuring that every person who seeks to contribute to our society can do so without fear of persecution or exclusion.

It is within our power to create a legacy that future generations will look back upon with pride, knowing that we chose love over fear, compassion over cruelty, and progress over impasse.

The time for action is now. Together, let us chart a path forward that embraces the transformative power of LOVE, and in doing so, let us create a nation that lives up to its promise as a land of liberty, opportunity, and prosperity for everyone.

Becoming Zophia

Becoming Zophia

Sophia was born in the Greece lands occupied by the Ottoman Empire at the time in 1710. She lived with her parents in a small village and witnessed the cruelty and oppression of Ottoman rule.

In 1712, when Sophia was just two years old, her parents decided to leave Greece lands and start a new life in the new kingdom of Great Britain. They journeyed to Britain to join Sophia's mother's Uncle and their side of the family, hoping to find safety and security.

Sophia's mother had always been the anchor that held their family together, the one who had kept them going through thick and thin. So, when news of her mother's injury reached Sophia, it was as if the ground beneath her feet had crumbled away.

Sophia's mother had been caught in the crossfire of a conflict that had erupted between the Scottish rebels and the British forces. She was just in the wrong place at the wrong time.

Sophia's father had rushed to her side, but it was too late. Despite the efforts of the doctors, Sophia's mother succumbed to her injuries.

The family's grief was compounded by the fact that they were already struggling to make ends meet. The famine had hit their village hard, and they had already lost much of their livestock and crops.

Sophia's father tried his best to provide for his children, but it seemed as if the world was conspiring against them.

Becoming Zophia

Sophia and her younger brother watched as their father grew more and more despondent. He was always a proud man, one who believed that he could provide for his family no matter what. But with the loss of his wife and the constant struggle to provide for his family, the sense of hopelessness that pervaded his every waking moment had taken its toll on him.

Sophia knew that something had to change. She couldn't bear to see her father suffer like this anymore. That's when she heard about the land of opportunity, Egypt. It was a place where a person could make a new start, where they could leave behind the pain of the past and embrace a brighter future.

Without a second thought, Sophia's family packed their few belongings and set out on the journey to Egypt. It was a long and arduous journey, but they were determined to start afresh. And when they finally arrived in Egypt, Sophia knew that it was the right decision. She felt a sense of hope that she hadn't felt in a long time, and she was determined to make the most of the opportunities that lay before her.

They settled in a small town near the Nile River, hoping to build a new life. Sophia, now sixteen years old, took on a new identity and became known as Zofia.

As they settled into their new life in Egypt, Zofia's father expressed his worries to her about their uncertain future.

Becoming Zophia

Zofia’s father lamented: "I know things have been difficult for us, Zofia, but do you think moving to Egypt was the right decision? What if we can't make a life for ourselves here?"

Zofia understood her father's concerns but reassured him, "We have to have hope, Baba. We can make a new life here. Look at all the opportunities that Egypt has to offer. We can learn a new trade, make new connections, and maybe even find happiness again."

Zofia faced many challenges in Egypt as a foreigner and a woman. She had to learn a new language and adapt to a new culture, and she faced discrimination and prejudice from some of the locals. But Zofia was determined to succeed, and she worked hard to learn the customs and traditions of her new home.

Zofia's father found work as a carpenter, and Zofia and her younger brother helped out by selling goods in the market. As they became more established in the community, Zofia began to make connections and build relationships with the locals. She learned about the history and culture of Egypt, and she developed a deep appreciation for the country and its people.

As she saw the impact of education on the lives of these young ones, she decided to pursue a career in education.

As Zofia began to focus on education and helping young teens, she faced criticism from some locals who questioned her abilities as a foreigner.

Becoming Zophia

The native yelled at her: "You think you can teach our children? You're just a foreigner who doesn't even speak our language," said one of the parents.

Zofia remained steadfast in her belief that education was crucial for these children's future and replied, "I may be a foreigner, but I am a qualified teacher who can provide a safe and nurturing environment for your children to learn and grow."

Zofia dedicated herself to teaching and helping children who had lost their families due to war or famine. She became a mentor and a guide for these young teens, providing them with a sense of belonging and a safe space to learn and grow.

Zofia's dedication and kindness did not go unnoticed, and she was soon appointed as a peace ambassador, responsible for fostering understanding and acceptance between different cultures.

When Zofia was appointed as a peace ambassador, she met with resistance from some members of the old-guard community who believed that peace was not possible: "Peace? Between us and them? It will never happen," said one of the elders.

Zofia patiently explained, "We have to try. We have to bridge the gap between our cultures and find common ground. We have to teach our children to accept and respect each other's differences."

Becoming Zophia

Her work was instrumental in building bridges between the immigrating community and the local population.

Despite the challenges she faced, Zofia never forgot her roots and remained proud of her Greek heritage. She continued to honor her mother's memory and passed on her legacy of resilience and determination to her own children and grandchildren.

As Zofia continued to make progress in her work, she shared her joy with her family, "Baba, look at what we have accomplished. We have made a life for ourselves here, and I am so grateful for the opportunity to help these young teens."

Zofia's father replied, "I am proud of you, my daughter. Your mother would be proud of the person you have become."

True Immigrant Values

True Immigrant Values

Immigrants bring with them a set of values that transcend borders and languages. These values, forged through resilience, determination, and the pursuit of a better life, form the foundation of our shared experiences as immigrants.

They remind us of our interconnectedness and the strength we derive from embracing diversity. As an immigrant myself, I have come to recognize and cherish these values that connect us together.

Hard work, embodied by a farmer sowing what they reap, is a value deeply ingrained in the fabric of our immigrant journey.

We understand that success is not simply bestowed upon us; it is earned through diligent effort and unwavering commitment.

Butterflies have shown time and again that hard work knows no boundaries, that with determination and perseverance, we can overcome obstacles and achieve our dreams.

Whether it's working multiple jobs to support our families or pursuing education while juggling responsibilities, Butterflies embody the spirit of hard work and inspire others to strive for excellence.

Education illuminates the path forward to success especially in uncertain times, and holds a special place in the hearts of immigrants. Butterflies recognize the transformative power of knowledge and the doors it can open. Education empowers the next generation with the skills and tools to succeed, broaden horizons, and navigate the complexities of a new world.

True Immigrant Values

That's why immigrant families emphasize this so much. Butterflies embrace the opportunities for learning, knowing that education not only enriches our own lives but also serves as a catalyst for positive change in society.

Family, like the sturdy branches of a tree, holds immeasurable value in the immigrant experience. It is a source of strength, resilience, and unwavering support.

For immigrants, family extends beyond blood ties; it encompasses the network of loved ones who offer a sense of belonging and security in a new and unfamiliar land.

Family provides a refuge in times of hardship and a source of joy in moments of triumph. It is through the love and sacrifices of family that Butterflies find the courage to embark on their journeys, knowing they have a foundation of care and encouragement to fall back on.

In the face of adversity, family stands as a beacon of hope, reminding us that we are never alone. The bond of family transcends borders, cultures, and languages. It embodies the essence of resilience, unity, and the unbreakable ties that connect us all.

Faith is the steadfast guiding light, holding profound significance in the lives of many Butterflies. It's an anchor providing strength, solace, and a sense of purpose. For countless individuals, faith is the bedrock of their identity, culture, and values.

True Immigrant Values

Butterflies often carry their faith traditions with them as they navigate the challenges of uprooting their lives and establishing new roots in foreign lands. Faith offers comfort and resilience in times of uncertainty, providing a sense of belonging and community. It fosters a spirit of hope, reminding Butterflies that they are part of something greater than themselves. It serves as a source of moral guidance, inspiring compassion, empathy, and a commitment to serving others.

Through faith, Butterflies find the courage to overcome obstacles, embrace new opportunities, and contribute their unique gifts to the world around them. It is a powerful force that unites diverse cultures and fuels the immigrant journey with unwavering determination.

These values of hard work, education, family, and faith shape our immigrant experiences. They empower us to overcome adversity, strive for excellence, and uplift those around us. As Butterflies, we bring with us a wealth of diverse perspectives and cultural richness, enhancing the fabric of our society. By upholding these values, we create a society that cherishes the potential and talents of every individual, regardless of their origin or immigration status.

Together, let us celebrate these values and advocate for an immigration system that honors them, creating a future where LOVE: Liberty, Opportunity, and Value for Everyone prevails.

Let's embrace these principles and set an example for the world, inspiring understanding, empathy, and positive change.

Thank You

Thank You!

I am filled with everlasting gratitude for your willingness to read my story and hear my case for a comprehensive immigration system that is rooted in love and liberty.

Whether you agree or disagree, partially or wholly I expect that you will be called into action and engage in this delicate dialogue for the sake of our collective future.

This book posed many questions and included activities for you to ponder and participate in. I encourage you to review them further, and if you feel compelled, share your responses with us at ButterfliesMoveFreely.com.

In fact, it would mean the world ot me if you joined the conversation online. Visit our website to share your story, join the membership, attend events and do what you will to help Butterflies Move Freely.

This book is just the beginning of a movement and my lifelong dedication to promoting a more inclusive and progressive social justice narrative.

Its up to you now.

Sincerely,

Elias Benjelloun

Collection of Quotes

Special Mention
George Santayana

Those who cannot remember the past are condemned to repeat it.

President
George Washington

The bosom of America is open to receive not only the opulent and respectable stranger, but the oppressed and persecuted of all nations and religions, whom we shall welcome to a participation of all our rights and privileges.

President
Abraham Lincoln

As a nation, we began by declaring that 'all men are created equal.' We now practically read it 'all men are created equal, except Negroes.' When the Know-Nothings get control, it will read 'all men are created equal, except Negroes, and foreigners, and Catholics.'

President
Rondald Reagan

I believe in the idea of amnesty for those who have put down roots and who have lived here, even though sometime back they may have entered illegally.

President
George W. Bush

We're a nation of laws, and we must enforce our laws. We're also a nation of immigrants, and we must uphold that tradition, which has strengthened our country in so many ways. These are not contradictory goals. America can be a lawful society and a welcoming society at the same time.

President
Bill Clinton

We should be increasing the number of legal immigrants, so that we can continue to build our economy and strengthen our families and communities.

President
Barack Obama

Are we a nation that accepts the cruelty of ripping children from their parents arms? Or are we a nation that values families? And works together to keep them together.

President
Barack Obama

Being an American is not a matter of blood or birth. It's a matter of faith. It's a matter of fidelity to the shared values that we all hold so dear. That's what makes us unique. That's what makes us strong. Anybody can help us write the next great chapter in our history.

President
Joe Biden

Immigration is essential to who we are as a nation, our core values, and our aspirations for our future.

Elias Benjelloun

I thought I was American, how did this happen?

Elias Benjelloun

I got a phone call and I felt my world and all my dreams shatter in an instant.

Mom

Your sister was detained by ICE and we need you now!

Elias Benjelloun

It is time to chart a new path forward, one guided by the values of LOVE: Liberty, Opportunity, and Value for Everyone.

Elias Benjelloun

Let us celebrate the colors, cultures, and contributions that Butterflies bring to society.

Collection of Quotes - Butterflies Move Freely
Sign Your Name Below

____

I declare my unwavering commitment to realizing this Dream of a United Humanity with Individual Liberty for All.

By nurturing interconnectedness and liberty, we create a world where every individual is recognized, respected, and valued.

Imagine how much more successful the process becomes when empowerment takes center stage?

When we concede and reduce to our greatest fears as human beings, unrelenting trauma & death follows.

Notes

Notes

Notes

Notes

Join The Movement

Butterflies Move Freely

Made in the USA
Middletown, DE
25 August 2024

59115802R00066